Preface...

Hello there! I'm Donna Sagen...

I started container gardening about 15 years ago after being inspired by one of my Master Gardener advanced training classes. The course was taught by the late Jim Wilson, a nationally recognized Master Gardener, and former co-host of the PBS show, "The Victory Garden". I was hooked right away, as I loved having planters full of color around my patio.

In 2005, I started Container Creations, planting full-scale container gardens for a handful of customers. The company has grown, and now we plant and maintain over 500 planters each spring and make seasonal changes as requested.

I LOVE my job and want to share my passion with others! Hopefully, you will feel my enthusiasm and get some useful information from this booklet!

Over the years, I have come across many different opinions on container gardening. I've been fortunate to be able to experiment and try virtually every plant available, so have great experience and knowledge to share.

While there are always new plants to try, I have stuck to the container gardening basics I learned back in that first class…because it works!

This booklet shares all of those basics…plus! I've included other things that are critical to a good container garden…plus design ideas, so you can create a comprehensive container garden that feels and looks great.

We are based in the Kansas City area, where growing conditions are challenging. All of the information in this booklet is suitable for most areas of the country, but may need to be tweaked for your specific area. Since we're in the middle of the country, most plants that we use can be used anywhere, but there are some really nice plants that we cannot use.

Check out our website at www.ContainerCreationsPlus.com for some nice combinations that you can duplicate. We also have a care blog with timely tips for keeping your containers nice all season and a forum for sharing your experience.

Enjoy!!!

Donna ☺

Table of Contents

Selecting New Planters

Planters can be expensive, so I like to put some thought into just how and where I'm going to use them. I prefer to use simple, permanent planters at the front door and then bring in some more fun and unique planters for other areas around the house. Shopping for them can be fun but also a bit over-whelming, as there are many choices.

The style and color at the front door should match the style and coordinate with the colors of your home. You can use the base color of the home or pick one of the accent colors, such as the color of the door or shutters. Either one works; it's really a personal preference...or what you find!

As for materials, here are some pros and cons of what's available. You should consider these when making your purchases.

Concrete

Concrete planters are best used in places that you want to have year-round color. I always recommend concrete for the **front entry**. Nothing lasts forever, but these will last for many years. In fact, it's the only material that can safely be left outside year-round. Concrete is also stainable, so you can get it in a color that complements your home. Even just a little aging color to concrete makes it much nicer.

Resin and Fiberglass

Fiberglass and resin planters are great because they are so lightweight and are now available in many shapes and sizes. Over time, the finish will peel, but you can get you several good years from them with good care. When you add a lot of pretty flowers to them, it's not always obvious anyway!

They're useful for tropical plants that need to come inside over the winter!

Clay

Classic planters in clay are available everywhere. While they look about the same everywhere, the quality ranges. The best clay is imported from Italy (of course!), and clay pots made in Italy will have that stamped somewhere on it; these will generally last longer (and cost more!) than the less expensive ones. Clay pots absorb water, so will require more diligent watering. This can be a negative, but also a positive...I have yet to see a plant in terracotta over-watered...*a very common mistake that kills plants*. Since clay is porous, these pots should be emptied and stored over the winter.

Glazed

Glazed pots are wonderful because they come in so many colors! Although they can be pretty heavy, most of them are still lightweight enough to move around when you want to. They make a great addition to your deck or patio where you can integrate some fun color!

Most of the glazed planters are only glazed on the outside, and the inside is left as bare clay. In these cases, the planters are as porous as clay and should be emptied and stored over the winter.

Iron

Iron planters have some good qualities: They can be left outside year-round, they last forever, and they are usually classically styled so go with most homes. But they can get VERY HOT if placed in the sun and the roots of the plants can literally bake! They also rust, so can discolor the surface where they're placed. For these reasons, *I don't recommend them*. If you already have some, move them into a shady area and use rubber risers to keep them off the ground.

Planter Placement Ideas

Creating a nice container garden is more than just planting a few pots and putting them randomly around your yard. You can create a comprehensive garden by placing your containers with purpose.

Try these ideas...

...Put your planters in little groupings around your deck and patio. This is a group of 3 terracotta planters, all different sizes. By combining all 3 together, the impact is much greater than any of them would be by themselves.

When selecting plants, *select plants for the whole group*, so they all look good together. Use the same colors or even one of the same plants in all 3 planters to pull them together. In this group, we used the exact same plants in the 2 pots on the ends and then used one of those plants in the center pot and repeated the white in a different trailing plant. It made a great trio!

...Vary your planters' shapes, materials and colors. Keep the planters at the front door classic and add some fun, colorful pots around your deck and patio. The flowers that you use should complement the colors of the pot.

8

...Use *Potrisers* and pedestals to keep pots off your deck and to add interest and height. You can find various pedestals at your local nursery, but I found some of these at the local craft and discount stores. Make sure you buy something that's sturdy enough to hold the pots...some can be very flimsy!

Potrisers are sold in some nurseries and online.

...Find spots with different **sun exposures** to add some variation to your plant selections.

...Use your planters to accentuate a focal point. *Planters that are scattered throughout the yard without any focal points create chaos and confusion.* Leave space between the groupings so the eyes can rest. **Large, single pots can work as a focal point** by themselves as long as you don't have too many of them. A nice tall grass moving in the wind can be a very nice eye catcher for a single pot.

Or something like this fabulous Plumbago that blooms all summer!

...Place planters to mask bland walls or to hide unattractive areas. And be sure to coordinate the flowers in the ground with your planters!

Determining Sun Exposure

Knowing your planter's sun exposure is critical to selecting the rights plants for it!

Some basic things about how the sun moves...

- The sun rises in the east and sets in the west.
- During the spring and fall, the sun moves roughly at a 55 degree southerly angle in the sky, so during these periods, the south side of you house will get more sun than the north side; During the summer, the sun moves straight overhead, so both the north and south sides of your house will get similar amounts of sun. When you are determining your sun exposure, use the *summer* sun exposure. The plants may take a little while to take off, but will be fine.
- The hottest part of the day is late afternoon, between 3:00 PM and 6:00 PM.

So, no matter where a pot is, if it's not covered directly overhead, it will get *some* sun. If it gets morning sun, it falls into the **Part Sun** category. If it gets afternoon sun, it falls into the **Full Sun** category.

Take a look at these examples...

First, let's look at *Full Shade*...

The pots are sitting on the porch on the south side of the house. The south side of the house does get more sun. However, since the porch is covered, and they are sitting back underneath the porch, they will not get one bit of sun. Therefore, they are considered *Full Shade*.

Now look at this part of the house...

There are 2 pots on the east side of the house. They will get direct sun until the sun moves just past the house and they will then be shaded by the house. The single pot up next to the house will get the same exposure, as it will get shaded by the tree. Therefore, they are considered *Part Sun*.

And the last exposure...

Full Sun

The remaining 3 pots on the deck and the 2 on the steps will have sun all day long, so they are in *Full Sun*. Since the afternoon temperatures are highest, planters will belong in this category *even if they only get a few hours of afternoon sun.*

Thrillers, Fillers and Spillers

If you've read gardening magazines, you probably have heard these terms before, but do you know what they are? They're catchy words that container garden enthusiasts have come up with so they can talk about their container creations!!! They *define* the role of the plant in the container.

Thriller - It's the main plant in the pot...usually the tallest one!

Filler - They're the plants that surround the Thriller...usually the 2nd layer in the container!

Spiller - They're the plants that hang over the edge of the planter!

Most containers have 1 thriller, plus a few fillers and a few spillers, but of course, there can be exceptions...

- Sometimes there is no thriller, such as in a hanging basket. Hanging baskets are usually just a lot of flowers that "fill" a basket and "spill" over the sides!
- Some plants make very nice containers as a single thriller...especially when using a small pot.
- Sometimes a plant will have 2 roles. A trailing type of geranium (as pictured in the example) creates a nice "filling" effect but also "spills" over the side of the planter.

Shopping...When, Where, What, How (Many), and Why?

Here are our suggestions:

When:

You want to be sure that you are past the last frost or you may end up losing some of your plants. You also want to be finished before it gets too hot. While there is nothing set in stone for either of these periods (especially here in Kansas!), we follow some general rules...after Mother's Day and before mid-June is usually safe, and outside of that, proceed with caution!

Also note that the plants that are available early in the spring are not the ones that are going to last all season in a hot climate. Many are cool season annuals and will be good until mid-summer.

Where:

Plants are expensive, and some varieties of plants are better than others. Reputable garden centers know and carry the best varieties...of everything you need. So, if you want to have the best chance for success, do yourself a favor and shop at a reputable garden center...at least until you get familiar with the plants. The big box stores carry a nice selection of plants and supplies, but you do have to be careful.

Garden centers are set up just like a grocery store. Annual flowers that grow in the sun are grouped together in one section of the store and annual flowers that grow in the shade are grouped together in another section. Perennial flowers are found in another section. So, if you know that your planter takes sun, then you can just to that section of the garden center to shop.

Of course, there are some plants that can go in both, but stay safe until you know those.

What:

- Plants: Starting with larger plants can be beneficial. We usually use 4"-5" plants. Occasionally we do use 4-packs, and less often 6-packs. When you use the smaller plants, the roots are also small and will need to be babied to ensure they survive. Also, when you start with the larger plants, your planter will look good as soon as it's planted.
- Potting Mix: Potting mix is available everywhere! Some are better than others, but you can make a nice planter with most brands if you follow some general rules…

  First of all, you want to be sure you use "potting mix" and NOT "potting soil" or "top soil". Second, try lifting the bag. A good potting mix is (relatively) lightweight. Third, many of them come with fertilizer in them; Skip those and add your own fertilizer so you know exactly what's in your planters. Fourth, some have water retaining crystals; Skip those too…It's way too easy to kill your plants by over-watering.

- Fertilizer: You need a slow-release fertilizer (like the brand *Osmocote*) that you can add to the potting mix when you are planting the pot. After that, you can add a liquid fertilizer (like the brand Miracle Grow) from time to time to increase blooms. Again, there are all different kinds on the shelves. Choose one with a higher nitrogen level, when possible. That's the 1st number on the bottle label that looks like this: XX-XX-XX.

How (Many Plants): is actually a personal preference. A planter can become full over time with just a few plants, but sometimes you will want to have a quicker flower display, such as in those planters that are placed at the front of the home. More plants allow you to bring in more color and texture, which can transform a "NICE" planter into a "WOW" planter. You may want to shoot for "WOW" at the front door and leave the simpler ones for other places around the home. Keep In mind that planters that are planted really full will probably require more maintenance to keep them from getting overgrown.

Why: Because who doesn't love flowers? ☺

Easy Plants for Beginner Success

Sun Plants:

- Angelonia (Annual)
- Bird of Paradise (Tropical)
- Coleus (Annual)
- Diamond Frost Euphorbia (Annual)
- Lantana (Annual)
- Majesty Palm (Tropical)
- Pentas (Annual)
- Salvia (Annual Varieties)
- Trailing Geranium (Annual)
- Walkabout Sunset (Annual)

Shade Plants:

- Anthurium (Tropical)
- Dragon Wing Begonia (Annual)
- Heuchera (Perennial)
- Hypoestes (Tropical)
- Ferns (All Varieties) (Tropical)
- Oxalis (Annual)
- Philodendron 'Xanadu' (Tropical)
- Shade Coleus (Annual)
- Torenia (Annual)
- Tradescantia (All Varieties) (Annual)

Part Sun Plants:

- Alternanthera (Annual)
- Bird of Paradise (Tropical)
- Caladium (Annual)
- Coleus (Annual)
- Creeping Jenny (Perennial)
- Dragon Wing Begonia (Annual)
- Impatiens (Annual)
- Torenia (Annual)
- Tradescantia (All Varieties) (Annual)
- Wire Vine (Tropical)

Check out our website at www.ContainerCreationsPlus.com to see lots of beautiful pictures of combinations that work well together. For ease of use, it's sorted by sun exposure and size of planter.

Color Matters

Colors are very useful in creating a particular feeling in your garden or patio area. By using different combinations of colors, you can set the mood to be energetic and exciting or calming and relaxing. So think about where the planter is going to be placed and think about the mood you want to set there. Then use these guidelines to create the effect you want.

Let's start by looking at three color wheels that will help you decide which colors to select...

The 1st color wheel shows COMPLEMENTARY colors. Complementary colors provide strong contrast between the plants and create an intense, exciting effect.

A 2nd color wheel shows ANALOGOUS colors. These are 3 colors that are consecutive anywhere on the color wheel. Using analogous colors creates serenity.

The 3rd color wheel shows TRIADIC colors. It uses a combination of 3 colors, with one as the dominant. It offers a little of both of the previous 2 color wheels by giving strong contrast but also harmony.

In addition to selecting colors that go well together, you should consider the intensity of color and the effects it will have on your setting. Bold colors generally excite the senses, and tend to grab our attention. Soft colors have the opposite effect, calming the senses and relaxing us.

Pick the color wheel that appeals to you and use it to select your plants. If you have a large pot, select multiple plants in the same colors.

Here are some pictures to illustrate how these colors can be used...

Complementary   Analogous

Triadic

The Planting Guide

Get Ready!

- *Check the weather*...If the weather service is predicting storms or high winds, you may want to hold off planting a day or so. Your plants come from a greenhouse that has perfect conditions for the plants and they need some time to acclimate to the real world! While it's preferable to shop and plant all in the same day, sometimes the weather doesn't cooperate! If you are faced with having to go ahead and plant in difficult conditions, just know that wind will dry out your plants so you will need to keep a closer eye on the soil. If the leaves get damaged, you can do a little pruning as you plant.

- *Gather your materials* (Use the checklist!)...

- *Prepare your pots*...You can go ahead and take care of this part before it's actually safe to plant.

  Make sure you planter is in the location it's going to stay **before** you plant it...Even plastic planters can get ridiculously heavy when planted!

  If there is old soil in the pot, empty it. *We don't recommend using old potting mix; start fresh in the spring!* **Why? Because** a) bugs and disease can over-winter in the soil and b) the soil compacts over time and loses its ability to drain well. Starting with fresh potting mix in the spring will prevent problems like these.

Clean the pot with diluted bleach. This isn't always necessary, but should be done routinely every couple of years, or more often if you had problems with the plants the previous year. If you don't remember if you did or not, go ahead and do it...Better safe than sorry!

Spread a **wet** paper towel over the hole. Cover the hole completely and press firmly before you add any new potting mix. Add a couple of handfuls initially to make sure it's not going to move. Then add the rest of the potting mix, up to about 6" from the top of the container.

Note: *Styrofoam and/or rocks are unnecessary! Sometimes adding a couple of large rocks is necessary if either your pot is very lightweight and you are planting a tree in it, or the hole at the bottom of the pot is exceptionally large (greater than 2"). **Other than that, it's a waste of valuable space for your plants' roots and can potentially cause problems.***

Press down the soil firmly with your hand to eliminate some of the air pockets. The soil will compact some when it's watered, so by doing this, you will eliminate the need to add more soil later.

Get Set!

- *Lay out the plants (*Use the planter layouts!*)...*

Go!

- *On to the planting...* Start by adding your slow-release fertilizer into the top few inches of the soil. Be sure to read the label and add the correct amount for your pot. While you can always fertilize later with a liquid fertilizer, this is fast and convenient and helps build strong roots! If you forgot it, you can add it later, but the sooner, the better...Healthy plants need food!!!

  Starting with the thriller plant, take each plant out and place them into the planter. To get them out of the pot, gently squeeze the container; they should lift out. If not, look at the bottom for roots that have grown through the pot and cut those off. If that doesn't work, you may have to cut the pot with scissors or a knife. Squeeze the roots before you put the plant into the planter. If the plant is root bound (really thick roots and very little soil left), use your knife to loosen them. Don't be afraid to do this; you really can't hurt them! This will help the plants get started rooting in their new home. Place them in the planter and then fill with soil around the plants, again pressing the soil firmly.

  Clean up the area before you water so you don't end up with mud!

Water *slowly* and *thoroughly (including the edges)*. For planters that are in full or part sun, water until the water comes out the bottom of the pot. For planters that are in full shade, water just deep enough that you are an inch below the bottoms of the plants' roots.

Sprinkler wands work well at gently dispersing the water over your plants. If you don't have one, put a finger in front of the hose or spout so the water doesn't all go in one spot.

Now, pour yourself a glass of wine or tea, sit back and admire your creation!!!

Materials Checklist

☐   Plants

☐   Potting Mix

☐   Fertilizer

☐   Gloves

☐   Paper Towel

☐   Serrated Knife

☐   Scissors

☐   Broom or Blower

☐   Watering Can or Hose

Planter Layouts

Square or Round Planter Placed Against a Structure

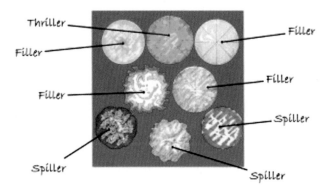

Square or Round Planter Placed In an Open Area

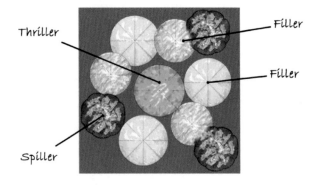

Rectangle Planter Placed Against a Structure

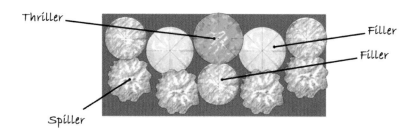

Rectangle Planter Placed In an Open Area

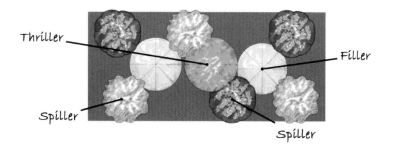

Hanging Basket

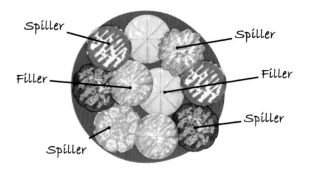

Basic Planter Care

Take care of your planters so you can enjoy them all season. At the very minimum, you need to water them, so make that a priority. Put it on your calendar so you don't forget! Pick a time of the day that works for you so it becomes routine.

In addition to watering, you will get more out of your planters if you take a little bit of time to take care of the plants. When taken care of, they can last all season long...until Mother Nature takes them with a frost or freeze! I would suggest that you spend a little time on a bi-weekly (every other week) basis. That way, you can address any issues that come up before they get out of control.

Watering

My new customers always ask me..."How often should I water?" My answer is always "When the plants need it!" Sounds simple, right? Well, it is!!! The plants need water when the soil is dry!

You'll want to check for moisture every couple of days at first. There's no better way to tell than by sticking your finger down into the soil! After a while, you'll figure out just how often you need to water and be able to have a fairly predictable schedule.

Once you determine that you need to water, the amount of water will vary, depending on the location of the planter.

For those in full sun, you water until it comes out the bottom of the planter. Make sure that you don't just water in the center of the planter either, but rather move the hose around so you include all the edges. I prefer to water with a spray nozzle with a shower head so the water is dispersed. If you don't have one, just put your finger in front of the hose while you water.

Shade is a little trickier because you only need to water a couple of inches below the plants' roots and stop. Again, you need to water around the whole surface of the pot.

Planters in **part sun** are watered like full sun...until the water comes out the bottom...but they won't need it as often.

When you water like this, you create deep, strong roots. Strong roots will help them withstand hot, dry summers and allow them to go longer in-between watering.

When you have first planted your pots, check on them every couple of days. If you've planted several pots and they're different sizes...in different sun exposures...you can be sure that their watering requirements **are not all the same.**

You can't water everything just because you have the hose out!

Later in the summer, you might be able to get your planters all in sync, but when the roots are small and the weather is cool, you can easily over-water.

In the beginning stages, over-watering and under-watering can actually look the same. Wilting leaves can mean either and only the person who is watering will have an idea of what is going on with the plant. Yellowing leaves are usually a sign of over-watering; Dry brown leaves are usually a sign of under-watering.

Under-watering can be corrected, but over-watering smothers the roots and they will die.

Does rain count? Yes and no. In the spring, it does because the roots are shallow and the plants are small enough that the rain gets into the planter.

Once the plants have grown and are covering the planter, the rain doesn't actually do much watering.

If you've combined tropical plants with annual flowers (as I like to do!), direct your water on the annual flowers, as they typically will use more water.

Planters placed in full sun really benefit from the consistent moisture of *watering emitters* connected to your sprinkler system but don't connect them until the cooler temperatures of spring are past. They are usually set to water automatically and that can lead to over-watering.

Deadheading

As a general rule, spent flowers should be clipped back to the 1st set of leaves. In addition to deadheading spent flowers, all damaged, discolored and dead leaves should be removed. Use small, sharp, inexpensive clippers for this task.

You will also want to periodically give some of your plants a haircut so they don't become overgrown. To give a haircut, lift sections of the plant and cut below the set of leaves of each branch, being sure to vary the lengths of each.

You never want to leave a straight, horizontal cut...but rather leave the plant in its natural shape!

Top layers of the plants are cut a little shorter to give a layered effect. This will expose more areas to the sun and therefore produce more flowers.

With a good haircut, the plants still look the same, only tidier...See the before and after sample on the following page!

Fertilizing

All plants need food to grow! Hopefully, you added the slow-release fertilizer when you planted your pot. (If not, you can add it at any time...just mix it into the top layers of the soil.) The slow-release fertilizers provide food for the plants over a period of time and save you the trouble of having to fertilize on a regular basis. The period of time ranges and is listed on the individual containers. Most of them say 4 to 6 months; however, the rate at which it is consumed by the plants is based on temperature (70 degrees) and moisture, so the label may be optimistic. In fact, here in Kansas, it only lasts about half that time!

The slow-release fertilizer should be added to your pots as it is used. Use the period on the fertilizer container as a guideline, and keep an eye on your flowers. Blooming will usually slow down when the food is used up.

In addition to the slow-release fertilizer, you can also use a liquid fertilizer from time to time, such as the brand Miracle Grow. Honestly, I don't use it often, but will if I'm preparing for a special event.

Pests

While there are many bugs that may find their way to your plants, there are only a couple of very common ones that we will address here.

Budworms are the larvae (caterpillar) of a moth and they eat geranium and petunia flowers...and that includes million bells which are actually just a smaller form of petunia! There's nothing you can do to prevent budworms because these 2 plants are hosts to them.

You have some options.

1) You can pick the caterpillars off the plants by hand

2) You can spray, or

3) You can just live with the damage they cause.

Spraying works best for minimal damage, but if you choose one of the other 2 options (more environmentally safe), your plants will be fine, but will go through periods without flowers.

For spraying, I use *Captain Jack's Deadbug Brew*. It's an organic product that uses a naturally occurring bacterium called *Spinosad*. The caterpillars die once they ingest the bacterium, so you only need to spray the buds and flowers. Since it has to be ingested, you will always have a little damage on the flowers.

I spray every 2 weeks, starting in June (when I see the first bites in the flowers) and into fall.

Spider mites come out when plants are stressed! They live in the soil and attack your plants when it is under stress. (Over-watering and under-watering are 2 sources of stress!)

Here is what it looks like:

You also may feel a sticky substance on the leaves.

Spider mites must be treated or they can kill the plant.

Again, you do have some options of which product to use. All products should be applied liberally, to both sides of the leaves…

- Insecticidal soap (or dish soap). You can use a wet paper towel and simply wash the leaves.
- Neem oil spray
- Insecticidal spray

Since I usually provide maintenance on a bi-weekly basis, I usually use the insecticidal spray. If you're looking for organic or a low toxicity means of control, the other sprays may be a better choice for you if a) you catch the mite early and b) you are available to re-spray on a tighter schedule.

Whichever option you choose, please read and follow the instructions on the label!

Fungal Diseases

We occasionally come across fungal diseases on our plants. It's usually caused by too much rain and periods of high humidity. Roses and impatiens are two flowers that they are most prevalent.

Black spot is a fungal disease that you may see on roses. It looks like this:

The leaves will eventually fall off, and although it will not kill the plant, it will make it unsightly. To treat this, you will need to spray with a fungicide. There are several fungicides available, but I use *Bonide's Copper Fungicide*. It's an organic product and it works well.

The fungal disease that you might see on impatiens is Downy Mildew. It looks like this:

After a while, the impatiens will lose their leaves and the plant will die. There is no treatment for this disease, so we just limit the number of impatiens we use in one place.

The disease is airborne, so the best defense against getting it is to buy your plants from a reputable nursery. A good nursery will take care to start with healthy plants and keep their eye on their stock so you are not sold infected plants. If your plants get this disease, you will definitely want to use fresh potting mix the next time you plant, as the disease infects the soil too.

Postface...

Hello again! I hope you've enjoyed reading this booklet and have gained some knowledge and good ideas for creating your own container garden.

I've tried to keep it all simple because when it becomes too complicated, it also becomes a chore. It should be fun and enjoyable and it should make you feel good. Even when I'm deadheading or spraying, I feel good when I see the results of my work! I hope that you will too!

Take time to enjoy your containers! Get out early and do your watering with a cup of coffee or in the evening with a glass of wine. Turn on some music and make it a time for you to relax!

Be sure to sign up for our care blog on our website...www.ContainerCreationsPlus.com. We will address other issues that come up that may not have been covered in the booklet. It's also a great place to ask questions and to share your own experience.

Share the passion!!!

Donna ☺

Made in the USA
San Bernardino, CA
19 January 2016